Eddie Swan was born and grew up in London, now living in rural Essex. He began writing short stories for his children when they were in primary school.

For my children; Jennie and Christopher, and my grandchildren; Jessica and Stella.

Eddie Swan

THE JOURNEY HOME

Illustrated by
Conrad Barnard

AUSTIN MACAULEY PUBLISHERS™

LONDON · CAMBRIDGE · NEW YORK · SHARJAH

A CIP catalogue record for this title is available from the British Library.

ISBN 9781398465602 (Paperback)
ISBN 9781398465619 (ePub e-book)

www.austinmacauley.com

First Published 2022
Austin Macauley Publishers Ltd®
1 Canada Square
Canary Wharf
London
E14 5AA

Whilst on a shopping trip with my wife, I spotted a small sign for sale in a shop window.

Family
Our refuge from the storm
Our link to the past
Our bridge to the future.
Anon

I have no idea who wrote it, but I certainly agree with the sentiments. My family are without a doubt, my world. So, I dedicate this story to my wife, my children, and my children's children. Also, all the dogs in our family, past and present, who inspired me to write this story.
First my daughter's two dogs.

'Penny' (sadly departed) a beautiful little white Westie. Impeccably behaved, devoted to my daughter, a constant companion through university and special arrangements allowed her to attend the church service, when my daughter got married.

Now she has 'Toby' a handsome rescue dog of mixed breeds. Was a bit of a rascal at puppy stage, but has matured into a loyal companion and a self-appointed guardian and protector to her two young daughters. Our beautiful and funny grandchildren, Jessica and Stella.

Last, but not least, my own two dearly loved, but sadly departed, dogs. A Labrador, 'Sam' and a golden retriever, 'Poppy'.

A dog's friendship is a wonderful thing, but when it's their time to go, they break your heart.

I once visited a medium, and the first thing she told me, as I sat down, was that I have two dogs by my side in spirit. She then informed me that they are with me, always.

Thank you, thank you, thank you, for reading my story, I hope you enjoy it.

Prologue

*"I believe that we are all travellers on a journey through life,
and if on that journey we find a true friend or loved one,
it should be considered a gift and a blessing from God and
the universe."*

Christmas Is a Wondrous Time

'Tis the season of hope, and good will to all. A time for giving, and forgiving. A time of expectation, and sometimes, the unexpected.

This is the story of a young boy called Christopher. He had been living away from home at boarding school. Now it was Christmas Eve, school had finished, and he was about to embark on a journey he would never forget.

He was making the journey home. Home was a ranching farm at the foot of the Rocky Mountains in North America. He lived there with his parents. When the snow fell in winter, it turned the Rocky Mountains, and vast forests of evergreen trees, into a winter wonderland. As the boy travelled home on the train, he sat looking out of the window at the picturesque landscape, and his thoughts returned to the day he had to leave for school.

Christopher's father was a good, kind-hearted man, who worked the land in summer, raising and harvesting crops for hay and feed grains for the horses, then tended to the livestock in winter. It was hard but rewarding work. Results often depended on the weather, so sometimes finances were a struggle. He often told his son, "If you want to get on in this world, and do good, you need two things; a good education, and a kind heart."

So, Christopher accepted his father's decision when he arranged for him to attend the best school that he could afford. But it was a boarding school in the city, which meant leaving home and staying at school, only coming home for the holidays. When the time came to leave, it was hard saying goodbye to his parents, but the hardest thing was saying goodbye to his best friend, Sam.

Sam was Christopher's dog. A golden retriever. Handsome, strong, gentle, and a loyal loving companion. Christopher and Sam had grown up together and were the best of friends. If one of them got into trouble, the other one was always there to help. Wherever Christopher went, Sam would be there right by his side. Christopher's mother would sometimes tease, "Honestly, you two are inseparable! Is there an invisible cord attached to the two of you?"

Christopher would always smile, give Sam a hug, and say, "Best friends forever! Right, Sam?"

As they all huddled together on the station platform, his father held Sam on the leash while his mother hugged him close. Struggling to hold back her tears, she told him, "Remember to treat others the way you would like to be treated yourself. But be wary of those who see this as a weakness. You know the difference between what's right and what's wrong; you're not a sheep, so don't let anybody lead you astray. Always be humble, and always be kind. It'll soon be Christmas, and we'll all be here, waiting for you to come home." With tears forming in his own eye's, he gave them both one last hug, then knelt in front of Sam.

Cradling his faithful friend's head in both hands, he gently massaged Sam's ears, Sam groaned with pleasure. Then, looking deep into Sam's eye's, he spoke gently to his best friend. "Now, you be a good boy, I'll be home for Christmas." Then he kissed him on the forehead, said goodbye and boarded the train. Leaning out of the window, he waved goodbye to them.

As the train pulled away, Sam strained at his leash, barking, and desperately trying to get to his friend. Christopher sat down on his seat, covered his ears, and sobbed.

Now, it was the holiday season, and Christopher was on his way home for Christmas. He had missed Sam and was hoping he would be there to meet him when he got off the train. He smiled to himself as he remembered back when Sam was just a roly-poly puppy, full of bounce and mischief! He chuckled when he remembered how Sam strutted around the place after he had saved up his pocket money and bought Sam a shiny new dog tag with Sam's name engraved on the front, made special by a second engraving on the back, 'Best friends forever.'

Suddenly, his thoughts were abruptly interrupted when out of nowhere came a woman's voice, "A penny for your thoughts dear?" Startled, he turned around to see who was talking to him. There, sitting opposite him, was a kindly looking older woman smiling at him.

"I'm sorry, what did you say?" asked Christopher with a puzzled look on his face.

Chuckling at his response, she repeated, "A penny for your thoughts dear?"

The woman was elegantly dressed and spoke with an English accent. There was something vaguely familiar about her, but he couldn't put his finger on it. She could see the boy was confused. Smiling warmly, she said, "Let me explain. It is an old English saying. When someone is deep in thought, so deep that they are oblivious as to what is going on around them, it is a polite way to get their attention and bring them back to their senses by offering them a penny to share their thoughts, and if they so wish, discuss what's on their mind."

The train journey was going to take some time, she seemed nice, and Christopher was glad of the company, so he said, "Sure, why not, my name is Christopher."

"Elizabeth," replied the lady, with a slight nod of her head. Then continued, "Pleased to make your acquaintance." Christopher smiled at her way with words, then he explained he was on his way home for Christmas and looking forward to seeing his parents again, especially his best friend Sam. He told her all about Sam. Recalling one Christmas Eve when he was younger, he had asked his parents' permission if he and Sam could camp outside under the stars overnight. His mother wasn't keen on the idea but agreed with certain conditions. So, he and his father pitched up a tent, built a log fire, then he, Sam, his mother, and father, all sat around the log fire with a cup of hot chocolate, supplied by his mother.

Then his father began to read them a Christmas ghost story called *A Christmas Carol* by Charles Dickens. "Oh, that's my favourite Christmas story!" said the woman.

"Good! You know it!" exclaimed Christopher. "It's sort of a family tradition now, we read it every Christmas Eve. \Anyway, when he got to the scary part about the first ghost, Jacob Marley, according to my dad, my eyes were as big as saucers! And at that very moment, an owl up in the tree above us hooted, and I jumped clean out of my seat! This startled Sam, he jumped up, my dad leaned back in surprise, his seat then balancing on its two back legs, slipped on the ice, and he ended up on his bottom in the snow, covered in chocolate!"

They both laughed, then Christopher continued, "Then my dad said perhaps we should continue the story inside. I agreed, then we all went inside and sat by the fireside. He finished the story, and I went to bed."

"And where did you end up sleeping?" asked the lady.

"In my own bed with Sam," replied Christopher with a wry smile on his face.

"You needn't be afraid of ghosts my dear," said the old lady. "After all, Jacob Marley came back to help his friend, not harm him. I believe we are all travellers on a journey through life, and if on that journey we find a true friend or loved one, it should be considered a gift and a blessing from God and the Universe." Christopher sat spellbound listening quietly to her words of wisdom. Smiling at him, she continued, "Animals are a good judge of character. Sounds to me like Sam loves you very much. You must have a kind heart to receive that kind of love. I can tell you love him very much. Love is a powerful thing. You can neither see it nor touch, but it is the most powerful force in the universe.

"My late husband was a reverend, at our little local church back home in England. And he believed that there is a place for the living, and a place for the dead, and that love, is the bridge that connects the two."

As the train gently pulled into the station, Christopher rubbed away the mist that had formed on the inside of the window. The snow was still falling. "Well, it's been lovely talking with you my dear, but I think this is your stop." Christopher jumped up in surprise.

"Oh!… you're right!" With that he quickly put on his coat and hat, picked up his bag, wished her a merry Christmas and hurriedly made his way to the carriage door.

"Wait!" called out the old lady. "You forgot this!" He rushed back, and the old lady pressed an old English penny coin into the palm of his hand. "A penny for your thoughts, remember? Keep it for luck!"

Christopher now smiled knowingly, thanked her, then put the coin in his pocket, and rushed back to the carriage door. Then it suddenly occurred to him, how did she know this was his stop? He had not mentioned where he lived. He turned back to ask her, but she was gone. Her seat was empty.

When the train finally stopped, he opened the carriage door and a sudden cold chill passed through his body making him shiver from head to foot. A thick blanket of snow had covered the ground, and as he stepped down off the train, the snow gently crunched beneath his feet. The snow was falling thick and fast, and the little country station seemed deserted. He closed the carriage door, and the train gently pulled away leaving him standing alone on the platform. He looked around for his mother who was supposed to be meeting him, but she was nowhere to be seen. The thick snow had formed an eerie silence. As he made his way over to the station masters office, the only sound to be heard was the snow gently crunching beneath his feet. He knocked on the door. No answer. He knocked again… still no answer. He tried the handle, it was unlocked, so he opened the door and went Inside. The little office was warm with a welcoming aroma of hot coffee that was brewing on a wood burning stove, that stood in the middle of the office. He called out, "Hello… is anyone here?" but there was no answer. Over by the window, there was an old brown wooden desk, with papers and books spread out in neat piles. Also, a telephone. He walked over to the desk, sat down on an old, worn out looking brown leather chair and picked up the phone to call his mother, only to find that the phone was not working.

"It's out of order!" came a sharp voice from behind him. He jumped out of the chair and span around to see the station master standing in the doorway, frowning at him.

"I'm sorry," said Christopher. "I was trying to phone my mother, she was supposed to meet me hear but—"

"It's the snow!" interrupted the station master. "It's blocked the roads and brought down the telephone line. They are trying to fix it, but I'm not sure how long it's going to take. It hasn't been as bad as this for years!"

He closed the door behind him, walked over to the stove and poured himself a hot cup of coffee. He looked over at Christopher and asked, "Would you like a cup of coffee?"

Christopher was tempted. "That does smell good, but I need to get home before nightfall. If the roads are blocked, there's no way my mother can pick me up, So, I guess I had better start walking if I want to be home for Christmas. If my mother manages to get through on the phone, would you be kind enough to tell her I'm okay and I'll be home soon."

The station master looked doubtful about letting him go and offered to let him stay until the weather improved. Christopher declined the offer politely. Then he buttoned up his coat, pulled his woolly hat on and down over his ears, put on his gloves, then picked up his bag, wished the station master a merry Christmas, then walked out into the cold bracing winter air. As he started walking, he could see his breath turning to vapour, as it met the cold air. It reminded him of something his mother always says, 'You know it's cold when you can see your breath!' The snow certainly brought beauty to the countryside, but it also brought danger. Animals that normally lived and hunted for food on high ground had come down to where the cold was not so severe. One of those animals was the wolf.

Christopher had been walking for some time when he stopped at a crossroads. The weather had started to improve a little, but he could not go any further on the road. The snow drifts were too deep, making the roads impassable. The only way to get home now seemed to be across country, but the snow had covered the land, this was going to make it hazardous.

He paused for a moment to study the landscape. He had to decide, should he risk it and venture across open country? Or should he go back to the station master's office and wait for the weather to improve? Then he remembered the penny coin. He removed his gloves and retrieved the coin from his pocket. Studying the coin, he said to himself, "You are supposed to bring me luck. Well, here goes. Heads we go back... tails, we carry on." Then he flicked the coin up into the air. Catching it with one hand, then smacking it onto the back of his other hand. Slowly he removed the hand that would reveal which side of the coin would decide his fate.

"Tails!" At that very moment, the snow stopped falling, a break in the clouds appeared and the sun came bursting through. He lifted his hand to cover his eyes from the bright sunlight when suddenly, he heard a dog barking. There in the distance, charging through the snow…was Sam!

"Sam?... Sam!" he yelled excitedly. Surprised, elated, and overwhelmed with joy, he ran to meet his friend. The snow glistened with all the colours of the rainbow as it sparkled in the afternoon sunshine. As they met, Sam jumped up to greet him, knocking him over into the snow! Over and over they rolled. Christopher laughing, and Sam barking. Tears of joy ran down Christopher's face and Sam licked them dry. They were together again at last. "Good boy Sam, I should have known you wouldn't let me down." It was then he noticed the snow had stopped falling, and he could clearly see Sam's paw prints in the virgin snow. He smiled when he realized all he had to do now was follow Sam's paw prints, and they would lead him all the way back home. Sam had come to guide him home!

As the two friends made their way home, Christopher was so happy, laughing and playing with Sam, he didn't notice he was being watched from a distance. Hidden amongst the forest of evergreen trees, was a lone wolf.

Eventually, once more, the clouds covered the sun. but the two friends were still having fun. Christopher made a snowball and through it high in the air for Sam to catch, which he did with ease, but the look of surprise on Sam's face when it disintegrated in in his mouth made Christopher laugh out loud. "Okay," said Christopher, as he picked up a fallen branch from a nearby tree. "Let's see you get this one," and he threw it as hard and as far as he could. As he watched Sam chase after it, he suddenly became aware of something behind him. He turned around, and there, waiting patiently for its chance to attack, was the wolf. As their eyes met, Christopher froze with fear.

The wolf's stare seemed to hypnotise the boy. Unable to move, he watched it edge its way, closer and closer. The wolf snarled showing its teeth. Its growl was low and menacing. Its hot breath turning to vapour as it met the cold winter air. Closer and closer the wolf came until he could smell the wolf's breath… then it pounced!

At that very moment, he felt something brush past his legs… it was Sam. Sam leapt at the wolf stopping it in mid-air! Both animals fell to the ground in front of him. Snarling, biting, and rolling around in a vicious fight. Christopher quickly came back his senses. He knew he had to help Sam, and fast!

Sam was a strong dog, but he was not as young as he used to be and certainly no match for a wolf. The wolf was a much larger animal and a natural predator, but that did not stop Sam from protecting his friend. Christopher quickly looked around, searching for something he could use as a weapon. Then he saw a large branch of a tree lying on the ground. He rushed over to it and picked it up, he could hear the vicious sounds of the fight going on behind him. He spun around and saw the wolf on top of Sam and was about to show no mercy.

Horrified, he burst into a rage, and with all the strength he could muster he rushed back, lifted the branch up high, and sent it crashing down onto the wolf's head!

The wolf fell silent and lay motionless on the ground. Panting hard, Christopher looked down at Sam lying in the blood-stained snow. Immediately sinking to his knees, he cradled his faithful friend in his arms. Fighting a losing battle to hold back his tears, he spoke gently to his best friend. "We did it, Sam… we beat the wolf!" Sam did not move.

"Please, Sam… please get up," pleaded Christopher. "We need to go home now." Sam still did not move.

Once more the snow started to fall. Sensing the urgency of the situation, he tried once again to coax his beloved Sam up onto his feet. "You need to get up now, Sam, because I'm not leaving you out here alone. Wolves normally hunt in packs, and there may be more around. I know you're hurt and you're tired, but you need to get up, please Sam… please get up!"

Sam still did not move. Huddled together in the cold snow, Christopher wrapped himself around Sam, using the warmth of his own body to keep his friend warm.

Christopher's eyes were tightly closed as he hugged Sam close and prayed hard for his best friend's recovery.

After what seemed an age, Christopher felt some movement. He opened his eyes and saw Sam's tail slowly wagging and thumping the side of his leg. Then he looked at Sam and saw him looking back at him! "Sam!" With a huge sigh of relief Christopher scrambled up onto his knees. "Can you get up, Sam? Can you get up for me?" Very slowly, Sam got up and shook the snow from his coat. He then sniffed and inspected the wolf. Satisfied that the danger was over, he looked at his friend and gave a soft bark of approval.

Christopher quietly laughed, surprised at his friend's reaction. Then he checked Sam's wounds. Again, to his surprise and relief, he discovered the wounds were only superficial. So once more, the two friends set off for home. This time Sam stuck close to his best friend's side. It was now late in the afternoon; the light was starting to fade, and darkness would soon cover the land. Suddenly, the quiet of the snow-covered countryside was broken by one of the eeriest sounds of nature… the howl of the wolf!

The two friends looked at each other, and without saying a word, they both quickened their pace. Neither of them wanting another encounter with the wolf.

Eventually they came upon a section of forest that was denser than they had previously encountered. The snow was not so deep under foot but clung heavily onto the branches of the trees. Christopher had an uneasy feeling as they entered the woodland.

Above them, he could hear the branches of the tree's creaking and groaning under the weight of the snow. As they made their way deeper and deeper into the forest, he came across a rabbit caught in a poacher's snare. Unfortunately, the rabbit had died trying to free itself, this saddened and angered him.

Christopher believed that killing animals for profit on their fur or sport, was simply unacceptable. If an animal had to lose its life for the sake of sport, then that was not sport!

But his thoughts were distracted when he heard a flapping sound. He made his way cautiously to where the sound was coming from, followed closely by Sam. To his surprise, he found a snow-white owl hanging upside down, caught up in the lower branches of a tree. As he got closer, he could see the owl had somehow managed to get its leg trapped in between two smaller branches of the tree that had grown too close together. The bird was clearly distressed and flapping franticly trying to free itself.

He instinctively ran over to help the bird. He tried to calm the bird by speaking softly, at the same time he took a branch in each hand and prized them apart by pulling with one hand

and pushing with the other. The branches parted and the bird fell to the ground.

Christopher knelt slowly and checked to see if the bird was okay.

Sam being nosey tried to edge his way a little closer to see for himself, but Christopher held him back when he noticed the powerful looking claws on the bird's feet. Owls are birds of prey with exceptional eyesight. They can spot smaller creatures on the ground while still in flight. Then swoop down, catch it, and carry it off to its nest to feed its young.

The bird seemed unharmed. It turned its head and looked at him, blinked its eyelids, flapped its powerful wings, then took flight. Flying low, it skilfully navigated its way through the trees, until finally, it disappeared.

Christopher paused for a moment, looked at Sam and said, "I thought owls were supposed to be smart!?" Then he got up, and once more, they both set off for home.

Eventually, they came upon a clearing. It felt good to see the open sky again. They stopped for a moment to take in the view before re-entering the forest. The clouds had moved on, the moon was full, and a carpet of stars covered the night sky. The moonlight seemed to reflect off the snow lighting up the whole area. "Beautiful," said Christopher. But as they moved forward to continue their journey, they were abruptly stopped in their tracks by what they saw standing directly in front of them. There, at the edge of the forest, stood the wolf! From the blood stains on its fur, they could see it was the same wolf they had encountered earlier. The wolf had regained consciousness and, like the natural predator that it was, it had picked up their scent and followed them. Circled around them whilst they were helping the owl and found the open ground to gain maximum advantage. Then waited until the two friends were out in the open, defenceless, with nowhere to escape.

Christopher felt vulnerable, there were no fallen branches at hand to use as a weapon. The wolf just stood there, staring, snarling, waiting to take its revenge.

His instinct was to run, but this was the wolf's domain. The wolf would have no trouble catching him.

Then he noticed Sam moving forward very slowly, then deliberately putting himself between him and the wolf. Horrified, Christopher tried to call Sam back. Standing like a statue, Sam had locked eyes with the wolf, and it looked like he was communicating with the wolf telepathically!

A flapping sound from overhead suddenly caught Christopher's attention. He looked up, and there, silhouetted against the moon in the night sky, flying above the treetops, was the very same snow-white owl that he had previously helped free from the tangled tree branches.

Then the strangest thing happened.

The bird perched itself on the very top branch, of the very same tree, that the wolf was standing under. The branch, already heavily laden with snow, bowed under the extra weight of the bird. Then, gripping the branch with its powerful claws, the bird began flapping its wings, and the branch began to shake.

The snow that had settled on that branch, suddenly slid off onto the branch below, which in turn forced that branch to release its own heavy load of snow. As the snow fell from one branch to the next, the snow gathered in volume and speed until a mini avalanche fell and landed directly on top of the unsuspecting wolf!

The wolf suddenly disappeared under a pile of snow, but almost as fast as it disappeared, came bursting up out of the snow! Shocked, startled, and disorientated, with its tail between its legs, it made a hasty retreat in the opposite direction.

Christopher seized the chance to escape and yelled, "Sam… run!"

The two friends ran as fast as could. They did not stop running until they cleared the forest and could see open sky again. Panting hard, out of breath but relieved to have escaped the wolf, Christopher collapsed down onto his knees, and with a look of disbelief on his face, he turned to Sam and yelled in astonishment, "Did you see that?!"

Christopher was having trouble believing what he had just seen with his own eyes. "Did that owl do what it did… on purpose? Or was it just a coincidence that the very same owl we rescued just happened to land on that particular branch, on that particular tree, that the wolf just happened to be standing under… at that particular moment?! If so, that would be one big coincidence!"

Christopher thought for a moment while getting his breath back, then said, "You know what, Sam? Maybe that owl is a lot smarter than I thought!" Sam gave his friend a knowing look, Christopher then looked up, and spotted way off in the distance, a light glowing in the dark. "Look, Sam… home!"

Once more, the two friends set off for home. Sam continued to stick close to his best friend as he guided him towards the light. As they got closer, Christopher could see that it was a large fire crackling and burning brightly, built with tree branches and logs. His mother must have managed to get through on the phone and found out from the station master that he was making his way home on foot. His father had made him a beacon of light, to help him find his way home in the darkness.

When he was close enough to see the warm welcoming lights glowing from the windows of home, and the smoke rising from the chimney, he suddenly threw all caution to the wind as the excitement of coming home overtook him. He started to run, but the snow was deep, and it disguised the unevenness of the ground below. He started yelling excitedly, "Mum! Dad! I'm ho…"

But before he knew it, he suddenly lost his footing, twisted his ankle and down he went! Unable to stop himself, he rolled down a riverbank, hit his head on a large rock by the water's edge, and rolled straight into the fast-flowing river that flowed alongside his home.

He passed out momentarily, but the icy cold water quickly brought him back to his senses. When he came to, he found himself alone out in the middle of the river, gasping for breath. He clutched at his travel bag and held on to it tightly, in the hope it would somehow keep him afloat. But his soaking wet winter clothes and heavy boots weighed him down and he struggled to stay afloat.

The sight of home was getting further away as the river carried him along. Disappearing completely when the current dragged him below the surface of the water. Fighting against the current, he managed to resurface, but he knew he could not stay afloat for long, he had only one hope. The ice-cold water had taken his breath away, making it hard for him to breath. But determination took over as he took a sharp intake of breath, then called out…

"S-S-SAM!"

With his strength exhausted, the river, swallowed him up. As he slowly sank below the surface of the water, into the murky depths below, he felt as if his lungs were about to implode. Suddenly, in the gloomy darkness, he felt a glimmer of hope, something was tugging at the collar of his coat, pulling him back up to the surface. As he resurfaced, the cold winter wind hit him like a slap on the face, instantly gulping in as much air as he could. Coughing, spluttering, freezing cold and exhausted, all he could do, was look over his shoulder, and there by his side... was Sam.

He had appeared out of nowhere and just in the nick of time. Swimming strongly against the flow of the river and dragging his beloved friend to safety. Christopher reached out and held on tightly to Sam's collar. As they reached the other side of the riverbank, Sam helped pull his exhausted friend out of the river. Christopher managed to hug and thank his faithful friend, before collapsing unconscious at the river's edge.

The next thing he knew he was being pulled to his feet by a pair of strong arms, it was his father. Christopher looked around and immediately asked, "Dad, w-where's Sam?"

His father noticed there was blood trickling down his son's face from a cut above his eye. He removed his own winter coat and placed it around his son's shoulders. "Never mind about that now son," said his father. "Let's get you inside by the fire."

Once inside his mother moved with speed and efficiency. She removed his wet clothes, cleaned the wound, prepared him a hot bath, and hung up his wet clothes to dry. She then gave him some dry clothes, a hot drink and sat him by the warm fireside.

Now feeling much better Christopher looked around the room and asked again, "Mom, where's Sam?" He looked at his mother and noticed there was a sadness in her eyes as she answered.

"Darling, there's no easy way to tell you this… Sam died two months ago!"

Christopher sat there staring at his mother, confused and speechless.

His mother continued, "Sam was a fit dog, but old age catches up with us all. When you left home to attend boarding school, that dog missed you so much. He went off his food, started moping around the place like a lost soul. Then one day he curled up on your bed, went to sleep… and never woke up."

Christopher's mind was reeling! "No!" he yelled. "That can't be!"

"I'm afraid it's true son," said his father. "We buried him out back under the blossom tree."

Unable to get his words out fast enough he spluttered, "That… that's impossible!" Then he told them the whole story. How Sam came to meet him at the crossroads. How he saved him from the wolf, their encounter with the owl, the return of the wolf… "And the river! What about the river!?" yelled Christopher.

"What about the river?" asked his father.

"Didn't you see?" exclaimed Christopher. "When I tripped and fell into the river, I would have drowned for sure! It was Sam that pulled me out, he saved my life!"

Now it was his parents that were confused and speechless.

Looking for some logical explanation his father asked, "You said that when you fell, you hit your head before rolling into the river?"

"Yes," replied Christopher.

"Well," continued his father, "maybe, you're not thinking too clearly at the moment?"

Frustrated, Christopher snapped back, "Then how do you explain how I managed to survive the river? I was frozen, exhausted, my heavy winter clothes and boots were dragging me under. I couldn't stay afloat; Sam was my only hope. I yelled for Sam and he appeared... out of nowhere! He pulled me back up to the surface! I held on tightly to Sam's collar, I knew my life depended on it! He kept me afloat and pulled me back to the river's edge. Sam saved my life!"

His father could see his son was getting upset, but he could see no logic in the story he was telling them. "When I found you at the river's edge, the only thing you were hanging onto was your travel bag."

Perplexed, Christopher turned to his mother. "Mom, you believe me, don't you?"

His father decided it best to try and calm the situation. "Okay son, I have to check on something in the barn. We'll talk more when I get back." With that, he put on his coat, pulled on his hat, and picked up his torch. As he opened the front door, a blast of cold air forced its way into the room. Then he walked out into the snow closing the front door behind him.

His mother placed her arm around her son's shoulders to comfort him. He looked into his mother's eyes, desperate for her to believe him. His mother chose her words carefully and spoke in a calm voice.

"I believe that right now, you believe, it all happened, just as you say it did."

"But mom!"

"The thing is," continued his mother, "if it really did happen the way you say it did, it would have to be some kind of.... divine intervention! In other words... a miracle!"

Christopher's parents had been dreading telling their son about Sam, so they had made some preparations. But no amount of preparation could have prepared them for what happened next.

The front door swung open, and Christopher's father came back into the room. Closing the door behind him, he removed his coat, and approached them with a look of bewilderment on his face. "What's wrong?" asked his mother.

His father spoke slowly, clearly mystified by what he was about to say. "I walked down to the river where I found Chris. I was looking for some sort of clue or explanation that might help solve this mystery, what I found was this." He held out his hand, he was holding a dog collar. It was Sam's collar! With Sam's dog tag attached. His name clearly engraved on the front. The very one Christopher had bought for him all those years ago!

His mother struggled to find some logical explanation, but then he turned the dog tag over. There on the back were the words… 'Best friends forever'. Now there was no doubt!

The three of them sat there in silence, staring at the fire, watching the flames dancing around the logs burning in the grate. Struggling to come to terms with, and understand, the events of the day, his mother spoke first.

"Well… I can't explain this, 'phenomenon'. I can only give you my opinion. You know that saying Grandma has about feathers?"

"Grandpa says Grandma has too many sayings!" interrupted his father. Both Christopher and his mother gave an amused knowing smile. Then Christopher added, "Grandma always says… your mother knows a lot of things, but your Grandmother knows more!"

"What?!" exclaimed his mother.

At this, they all laughed! With the tension beginning to ease, his mother continued, "I was referring to the saying she has about white feathers?" Both Christopher and his father had blank looks on their faces. "Clearly you don't," said his mother. "Let me refresh your memories.

"Grandma says… 'White feathers appear when angels are near'.

"I mention this because when I hung your wet clothes up to dry, I found a white feather in your belongings. Now you could be forgiven for thinking, it's probably a white feather from that owl, but I found it inside your travel bag, and the bag was tightly secured. So, unless you put it there?"

"No!" replied Christopher.

"That's what I thought," said his mother.

"So, after hearing your incredible story, I think that there is only one explanation. What you experienced today… was a miracle!"

She paused for a moment to let what she had just said sink in. Then continued, "It's my belief, that the universe has powers that we are only just beginning to discover. The universe has given you a truly precious gift today.

"The law of attraction says that like attracts like. You helped that owl, that owl helped you. Kindness and love attract more kindness and love. You have a kind soul, my boy, and the love that you and Sam have for each other is so strong, it seems that nothing can break it, not even death!

"I believe that some of us are blessed with a guardian angel watching over us. Guiding, and protecting us when we need it most. That dog loved you so much that somehow, he came back today because he knew you were going to need his help. I think we know who is watching over you.

"Sam has given us hope today, and proved that real love never dies."

Christopher's eyes filled up with tears, and with tears forming in his mother's eyes, she hugged him close, and that was when he saw it. Looking over his mother's shoulder, he noticed an old black and white photograph in a frame, standing on the mantle shelf above the fireplace. it was a photograph of an elegantly dressed elderly lady.

There was a soothing tone in his mother's voice, but her words were not clear. He was now focused on the photograph. Suddenly, Christopher blurted out, "It's her!"

"What? Who?" asked his mother.

"This is the lady I met on the train!" exclaimed Christopher. "I thought she looked familiar!"

"No, that's impossible, this is your great grandmother, Elizabeth. She died before you were born!" explained his mother.

Christopher was undeterred. "I'm telling you I met her on the train today. She was well-dressed and had an English accent. I remember she had a warm friendly smile and just like Grandma she had this funny little saying." Christopher thought for a moment, and then began, "A penny for—" but before he could finish the saying, his mother joined in, and they both finished it together, "Your thoughts dear?"

Taken by surprise, Christopher looked at his mother for an explanation. "She used to say the same thing to me when I was a young girl!" said his mother. "Whenever she caught me daydreaming, she would say, 'A penny for your thought's dear?'"

His mother then went on to explain how she came across the old photograph whilst looking for the Christmas tree decorations in the loft. "It was with that book she gave me for Christmas, years ago... *A Christmas Carol* by Charles Dickens.' I had an old English penny that she gave me," continued his mother. "I keep them all together, but the coin has disappeared."

Christopher walked over to his coat that was hung up to dry. Searching through his pocket, he pulled out the penny coin she had given him. His mother gasped with shock! "That's the penny she gave to me all those years ago. She told me to keep it for luck."

"She said the same thing to me," said Christopher as he handed his mother the coin. "Then she disappeared! She told me something else," continued Christopher,

"I thought it a little strange at the time, but now it makes perfect sense. She told me she had a late husband who used to be a reverend at their local church back home in England. And he believed that there was a place for the living, and a place for the dead, and that love was the bridge that connected he two."

Christopher's mother was now lost for words. With all the strange events of the day whirling around inside her head, she began to feel a little dizzy and had to sit down.

His father, who had remained silent listening to all the revelations that were unfolding, stood up and slowly walked over to his wife and placed an arm around her shoulders. Speaking in a soft voice he said, "I think this is what they call, 'A Christmas Miracle'. Son, your mother and me have been married for more years than I care to remember, and in all this time, I have never, and I mean never... seen your mother speechless!"

At this revelation, they all burst out laughing! "Well, I was going to say... 'A penny for your thoughts dear?'" continued his father.

"Oh, stop it!" said his mother still laughing. "I think it's time for bed."

His father paused for a moment and then asked, "Does this mean we are not going to read *A Christmas Carol* tonight?"

His mother looked at his father, and with one eyebrow raised, she retorted back, "I think we have had enough ghost stories for one night!"

As they made their way to bed, a feeling of sadness descended upon Christopher, as the realisation that he had lost his best friend began to sink in. "Mom, will I ever see Sam again?"

She looked at her son and saw the sadness in his eyes. She then placed Sam's collar and dog tag in his hand and said in a gentle voice, "I think Sam is going to be with you always."

"Remember that invisible cord I used to tease you and Sam about when you were younger?" Christopher nodded his head. "That... 'invisible cord' is the true friendship and love that you and Sam have for each other, and it's still there. You may not be able to see him physically, but he's with you, as always... in spirit."

When Christopher awoke the next morning, it was Christmas Day. His parents had let him sleep in late. He got up, put on his dressing gown, and shuffled sleepy eyed into the living room. His father had lit the fire; it was a welcoming sight. He settled himself in the armchair next to the fireplace. As he watched the fire softly burning, the smell of freshly brewed coffee and toast began to waft in from the kitchen, it felt good to be back home again.

Gazing into the flickering flames, he started to reflect on the journey home.

Suddenly, his parents came bursting into the room full of excitement. "Happy Christmas, sleepy head!" He looked up to see them both standing in front of him, big smiles on their faces, and in his father's arms sat a Golden retriever puppy!

His father placed the puppy onto Christopher's lap. Feeling a little unsure of how he was going to react to the puppy, given all that had happened the day before, he spoke in a tentative manner.

"We hope," said his father, "you can forgive us for not telling you about Sam sooner. We knew you would be heartbroken, and there was nothing to be gained, telling you while you were miles away at school. So, we have had this planned for some time. We know that no dog can ever replace Sam. But we thought she might help soften the blow. For us too. The place just seems so empty without Sam.

"All you have to do is pick a name for her." Christopher's heart melted at the sight of the little puppy and the puppy took to Christopher instantly. Climbing up his chest and licking his face with her tail wagging so fast, he had trouble holding her!

Laughing at the little bundle of mischief, he paused for a moment and then said, "I think I have the perfect name for her. You said last night that Sam had given us hope, so why don't we call her… 'Hope'?"

"Perfect!" said his parents. "Happy Christmas, Hope!"

As Christopher sat there surrounded by the warmth and love of his family, he knew he would never have made it home without Sam, and the true friendship and love that he and Sam shared really was… a gift, and a blessing.

Epilogue

And so it was agreed, a new life and a new 'Hope' had entered all their lives. Christopher built a new loving friendship with Hope but never forgot his journey home with Sam. He kept Sam's dog tag with him always, as it made him feel close to his best friend. When he came home for the holidays and sat in the armchair by the fireside, Hope would sit beside him and rest her head on his knees. As he massaged her ears the way he did for Sam, she would groan with pleasure, just the way Sam did, and sometimes, he had the strangest feeling. When he looked deep into her eyes, he felt he could see the spirit of Sam, looking back at him, with that happy smiling expression on his face that he missed and loved so much.

Christopher went on to prove his father right. He worked hard at school and got a good education. Then went onto university, where he teamed up with a fellow student and did good by starting up a training school for guide dogs for the blind.

He called it… 'Guardian Angels'.

His mother kept the white feather and had it framed with an inscription below.

'White feathers appear when angels are near'

The End.